Heroic Dogs

MILITARY DOGS

by Dale Jones

Consultant: Ron Aiello, President
United States War Dog Association, Inc.

BEARPORT
PUBLISHING

Minneapolis, Minnesota

President: Jen Jenson
Director of Product Development: Spencer Brinker
Senior Editor: Allison Juda
Associate Editor: Charly Haley
Designer: Colin O'Dea

Library of Congress Cataloging-in-Publication Data

Names: Jones, Dale, 1990- author.
Title: Military dogs / by Dale Jones ; consultant, Ron Aiello, President, United States War Dog Association, Inc.
Description: Minneapolis, Minnesota : Bearport Publishing Company, [2022] | Series: Heroic dogs | Includes bibliographical references and index.
Identifiers: LCCN 2021007356 (print) | LCCN 2021007357 (ebook) | ISBN 9781636911168 (library binding) | ISBN 9781636911250 (paperback) | ISBN 9781636911342 (ebook)
Subjects: LCSH: Dogs--War use--Juvenile literature.
Classification: LCC UH100 .J66 2022 (print) | LCC UH100 (ebook) | DDC 355.4/24--dc23
LC record available at https://lccn.loc.gov/2021007356
LC ebook record available at https://lccn.loc.gov/2021007357

For more information, write to Bearport Publishing, 5357 Penn Avenue South, Minneapolis, MN 55419. Printed in the United States of America.

Contents

All Clear! 4

Four-Legged Recruits 6

Canine Training. 8

Living on Base 10

Staying Safe 12

On the Front Lines 14

Bomb Sniffers 16

Paws on Patrol 18

Rest after Service. 20

Meet a Real Military Dog 22

Glossary. 23

Index 24

Read More 24

Learn More Online 24

About the Author 24

All Clear!

A group of soldiers is ready to enter a building ahead, but they need to be sure it's safe. Sounds like a job for a military dog! The **canine** soldier puts its nose down and gets to work. It sniffs for enemies and bombs. When the military dog **signals** that it's safe, the human soldiers move in and get to work.

Military dogs work all around the world. In the United States military, these dogs are officially known as military working dogs, or MWDs.

Military dogs will often lead the way so that they can detect danger and keep others safe.

Four-Legged Recruits

Being a MWD is hard work. Not every dog is up for the job. Military groups look for puppies that show promise from an early age. They want dogs that are smart and can stay **focused** in loud or busy places. Military dogs also need a strong sense of smell.

German shepherds, Dutch shepherds, Labrador retrievers, and Belgian Malinois are often picked to start training to be military dogs.

Some puppies are born for the job! They are cared for by members of the military until they can begin training.

Canine Training

Once pups prove they're made of the right stuff, they start with basic training at Lackland Air Force **Base** in San Antonio, Texas.

Basic training for military dogs takes four months. During this time, each dog lives and works with a **handler**—the soldier who will be its partner.

Military dogs run through obstacle courses during their training.

After finishing basic training, some dogs practice sniffing for bombs or weapons. Other MWDs learn how to search for people or dig tunnels. Still others train to rescue soldiers in danger.

Living on Base

Next, it's time for handlers and their dogs to ship out. These teams can be **deployed** to bases around the world. While on base, MWDs have important jobs to do almost every day. They also practice with their handlers often to keep their skills sharp.

Handlers feed their dogs and clean their kennels every day. They also give the dogs regular baths.

Handlers care for their dogs so that they are ready when duty calls.

Staying Safe

All soldiers need gear to stay safe on the job. This includes military dog soldiers, too. MWDs often wear special vests, boots, or goggles for **protection**. Military dogs might also carry lights, radios, and other supplies.

Military dog vests typically weigh anywhere from 3 to 7 pounds (1.4 to 3.2 kg).

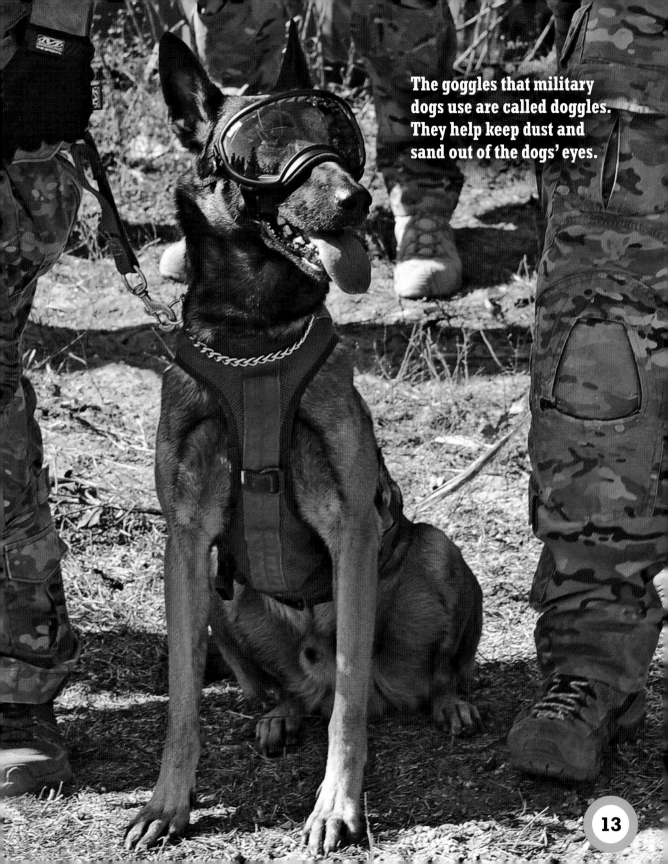

The goggles that military dogs use are called doggles. They help keep dust and sand out of the dogs' eyes.

13

On the Front Lines

Once they're all geared up, military dogs go out on missions! Sometimes, they are sent ahead of other soldiers to make sure an area is safe. They may have cameras and radios attached to their vests. Then, handlers can see what is happening and give the dogs commands.

The gear a military dog wears depends on the type of mission it's on.

When MWDs head out on a mission, they may ride in helicopters. Some of them even jump out of planes with their handlers!

Bomb Sniffers

Working on the front lines can be dangerous. Military dogs who sniff for bombs are specially trained. When MWDs find the scent of a bomb, they **alert** their handlers by sitting down. Then, the soldiers find a safe way to **disable** the bomb or go around it.

Bomb-sniffing dogs are trained not to touch anything they find. Touching a bomb might cause it to go off.

Humans have not come up with anything else that can find bombs as well as dogs can.

Paws on Patrol

Bombs on the front lines are not the only danger that military dogs sniff out. Some MWDs protect military bases with their super smelling noses, too. They **patrol** bases with their handlers and alert them if they see, smell, or hear anything strange. An early warning of danger can save lives.

A dog can use each nostril on its own. This tells the dog which direction a smell is coming from.

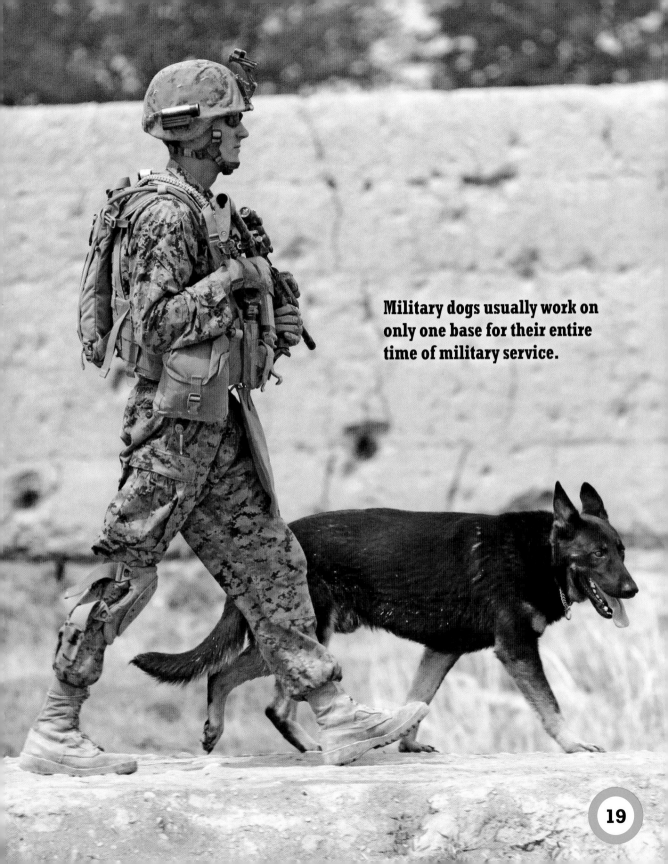

Military dogs usually work on only one base for their entire time of military service.

Rest after Service

Military dogs spend much of their lives working. Most of them **retire** when they're between 10 and 12 years old. Retired military dogs often spend the rest of their lives with their handlers or their handlers' families. After years of hard work, they deserve peace and rest.

The U.S. War Dog Memorial in New Jersey honors the work of all U.S. military dogs.

Retired military dogs are often celebrated
as veterans wherever they go.

Meet a Real Military Dog

U.S. Army Sergeant Nathan Arriaga and his partner, Zzar, work together as a team. Zzarr patrols and sniffs for bombs, and Nathan helps show him where to search. When Zzarr works off leash, Nathan uses hand and arm signals to tell his partner what to do. Together Zzarr and Nathan have successfully found bombs and other weapons. The work they do helps save lives.

Zzarr's name has two *z*'s because all puppies born at Lackland Air Force Base have names that start with double letters.

Glossary

alert to get a person's attention by touching, barking, or another action

bases places where soldiers live or operate from

canine a dog

deployed sent to an area for a specific purpose

disable to make something not work anymore

focused keeping full attention on one thing

handler a person who helps to train or manage a dog

patrol to watch or travel around an area in order to protect it

protection something that keeps someone or something safe

retire to stop working, usually because of age

signals sounds or movements that tell someone something

Index

alert 16, 18

base 8, 10, 18–19, 22

basic training 8–9

bombs 4, 9, 16–18, 22

gear 12, 14

handler 8, 10–11, 14–16, 18, 20

helicopters 15

Lackland Air Force Base 8, 22

mission 14–15

patrol 18, 22

retire 20–21

supplies 12

Read More

Gitlin, Marty and Katie Gillespie. *Military Dogs (Dogs with Jobs).* New York: AV2 by Weigl, 2020.

Holmes, Parker. *K9 and Military Dogs (Canine Athletes).* Minneapolis: Abdo Publishing, 2019.

Learn More Online

1. Go to **www.factsurfer.com**
2. Enter "**Military Dogs**" into the search box.
3. Click on the cover of this book to see a list of websites.

About the Author

Dale Jones lives in Los Angeles, California, with his family and two dogs.